T0198690

MEMORIES
OF
EXOTIC KENYA

A Ten-Year-Old's Perspective

SARAH KHAN

WestBow Press books may be ordered through booksellers or by contacting:

WestBow Press
A Division of Thomas Nelson & Zondervan
1663 Liberty Drive
Bloomington, IN 47403
www.westbowpress.com
844-714-3454

ISBN: 978-1-6642-6950-7 (sc)
ISBN: 978-1-6642-6951-4 (e)

Library of Congress Control Number: 2022911429

Print information available on the last page.

WestBow Press rev. date: 03/09/2023

WESTBOW
PRESS®
A DIVISION OF THOMAS NELSON
& ZONDERVAN

CONTENTS

ACKNOWLEDGEMENTS

I want to dedicate this memoir to my mom and dad and to my loving family, which is all of you. I would especially like to thank Aunt Naz, who inspired and motivated me to put my thoughts and experience during our trip to Kenya, together into this writing.

Aunt Naz, a seasoned teacher and my mother's sister, is a source of constant positive motivation, love, and encouragement.

I hope that you too will share and enjoy my experience with the wild animals and the fascinating land of wonders.

CHAPTER 1
Flying to Kenya

It was ten o'clock the night of July 26, 2019. I was in bed and was supposed to be asleep. My eyes wouldn't close as I counted the hours before we would be in the air. I lay there, imagining what was to come on this long-awaited trip to Kenya. I have always wanted to visit this incredible land of sun, beauty, and outstanding national parks.

Kenya is located in East Africa, averaging a distance of 7,350 miles from New York. It would take at least 12 hours or more to get to Qatar and another 5 and a half hours to reach Nairobi, the capital city of Kenya.

I have traveled with my family, including my aunt, uncles, and cousins to various parts of the world. In 2018 we all traveled and toured Italy, France, England, and Turkey. 2019 was going to be the year to visit Kenya.

This exotic land of the Maasai, Kikuyus, Luhya, and other tribes held a very special place in my heart since it was my mama's birthplace. The trip would facilitate another family holiday and fulfill my mother's wish to revisit the memories of her childhood in Kenya. I wanted to experience and see everything that my mother had once seen for myself. It was going to be special since my two cousins, Ariana and Inaya, would also be on this journey. Ariana and Inaya are sisters but their love, support and friendship means more to me than that a sibling could offer. We are after all the ASI sisters incorporated.

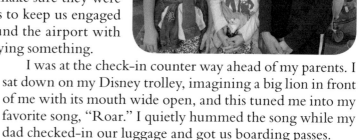

At exactly six o'clock the next morning, I woke up with excitement and started to get all my last-minute items into my backpack. A few hours later, I was at John F. Kennedy International Airport, where I had taken so many flights before to different parts of the world.

The ASI sisters checked their backpacks to make sure they were loaded with different games, candies, and books to keep us engaged on this very *long* flight. We were running around the airport with uncontrollable excitement, and everyone was saying something.

I was at the check-in counter way ahead of my parents. I sat down on my Disney trolley, imagining a big lion in front of me with its mouth wide open, and this tuned me into my favorite song, "Roar." I quietly hummed the song while my dad checked-in our luggage and got us boarding passes.

Finally, we all boarded the plane. ASI got a whole three-seat row to ourselves, and the fun began. We checked out other passengers who were sitting in front, behind, and across the aisles from us and realized we were the only kids.

My dad, who is my hero and favorite person, was even more the reason for my excitement. Not only has he traveled to Kenya before and probably knows every nook and corner, but he is also funny, smart and a lot of fun to be with. He could easily have been our official tour guide.

I have a sweet ritual for every flight with my dad. My dad and I always pretend to be pilots and hold the seat armrest as if it were the pilot's joystick, and we would lift it up slowly as the plane rose to make us believe that we were flying the plane.

So, I excused myself and went to sit next to my dad for takeoff. The plane started to speed up on the runway, and then my dad and I flew it off into the sky. I was still smiling from this excitement when I returned to my seat after the seat belt sign was turned off.

We played board games and read to each other, and before long, each one of us was watching a favorite movie.

ASI was already imagining what the next leg of this journey would be like when we had a stopover in Qatar. Hmmm, I was dreaming about Qatar Airways' food, which had never disappointed me before. I may have even dozed off a little. Time ticked away, and after a fourteen-hour flight, we landed at the Qatar airport. The ASI sisters were a sight to see. We looked like rag dolls.

The adults were attracted by the strong aroma of Costa coffee, while the kids gleefully feasted on chocolate donuts. There was an announcement calling our names to report to gate D for boarding. We gobbled our snacks, grabbed our backpacks, and were just making a dash to the gate when Uncle Amir exclaimed, "Has anyone seen my wallet?"

Uncle Amir, Farina's husband and dad to Ariana and Inaya, chose to be the cameraman for this trip. He is a very hands-on type of person who is gentle, humble and always most helpful. He had purchased a very high-tech device that took breathtaking views. This would not be the first time though, that his wallet went missing...

"Uncle, I saw you handing out your card to the lady at the counter," I said.

"Baba, I hope you did not leave it at the counter!" cried Ariana.

Farina was extremely anxious and remarked, "Not again!"

Farina is my mother's niece who also grew up in Kenya. Although there is a huge age gap between Farina and I, she and her brother Nabeel (Mamu) are on my list of best buddies, siblings, and many other meaningful relationships rolled into one. They are two of the sweetest people on earth, and I hope you will also come to love them as I do when you read my memoir.

Uncle Hamid (Nana) urged us all to carry on to the boarding gate and reassured us that all would be fine. Nana is my mom's older brother. He is like a sweet grandpa I never knew and has the gift of a golden voice. He is talented, loving, kind, and very knowledgeable about science and especially music. I love to hear him sing Elvis songs on the guitar. I was thrilled to have him with us all on this memorable journey.

Uncle Amir soon joined us with his pleasant smile, holding up his wallet. I felt like running through the security gate and getting straight on to our flight.

Soon we were back in the sky flying to Kenya, my dreamland.

CHAPTER 2
Arrival in Nairobi

July 28, 2019

As the wheels touched the runway of the Jomo Kenyatta International Airport in Nairobi, I felt my heart would explode with emotions. It was not as grand an airport as JFK in New York or Hamad International Airport in Qatar, but there was something special that I immediately connected with. These feelings grew stronger as we moved forward. The tropical breeze and the sunny afternoon were hypnotizing.

The minibus driver was waiting for us, and soon after the baggage was cleared, we were driven to IBIS, a boutique hotel near the center of the city. IBIS is a small hotel that is popular among tourists due to its location providing easy access to malls and the city, fine ambience, and very pleasant staff.

I loved the Swahili greeting by the most elegant and pretty receptionist. With her ever-nice smile, she said, "*Jambo, karibuni.*" When translated to English, this means, "Hello, welcome!"

My tongue rolled a little, but I managed to say "*Asante sana*," meaning, "Thank you very much," as I had learned from my pocket tourist guide.

After an hour's rest, we were driven to my Aunt Pini's house for dinner. This was going to be my first time meeting her in Kenya. Aunty Pini is Nana's wife who visits him in New York. She holds an executive position with a private airline and is stationed in Nairobi. I had heard about her excellent cooking skills and her sweet personality. When we arrived at her house, she was on the patio waiting to greet us with a large smile. Her house was decorated in classic tones with bright Persian rugs and artifacts from different countries. As I looked around, I found familiar objects, including a tapestry from Turkey, which reminded me of our trip to Turkey in 2018. There was a Russian samovar sitting right in the center of Aunt Pini's hutch, which reminded me of the one my mother had purchased when she was a medical student in Russia.

I asked Aunty Pini, "Did you also travel to Russia?"

She sweetly touched my cheek and said, "My child, I am waiting to travel with you and your parents since they both know the language and the country so well." She then continued with a twinkle in her eye, "They can be our tour guides."

I knew I would enjoy being there. Some of my mother's cousins had also joined us for this dinner, and everyone could not stop hugging each other and especially us, the kids. I thought, *I could get used to this.*

Dinner was a grand affair with very authentic national delicacies that my Aunt Pini had prepared especially for us. It was all like a big dream, and the ASI sisters were soaking it all in. Inaya was engaged in a silent conversation with her Barbie. Back in New York, Inaya has a collection of over 120 Barbie dolls. Ariana chatted with Aunt Pini while they ate dessert. Although everyone was exhausted, no one wanted any of this to end, but it was getting late, and we had to be up early for the next leg of our journey.

July 29, 2019

After an elaborate breakfast, which was a mix of local fruits, pancakes, chocolate croissants, and hot chocolate, we were delighted to meet the very energetic and friendly drivers, John and Alfred, with their two safari SUVs that had a partially open roof and large glass windows. The two men were going to be important figures of our safari. John and Alfred were both experienced wild safari drivers and had excellent knowledge of the geography and African wildlife.

We were briefed about the journey ahead and also presented with safari hats and Maasai blankets. Everyone scrambled to find a favorite seat in one of the two SUVs. I sat with my two cousins, Uncle Amir, and Dad in the vehicle driven by John. Finally, it felt like my African dream safari had begun, and I was now on my way to explore unimaginable places. There was so much excitement that my head felt dizzy!

As we drove out of Nairobi, the tarmac road slowly gave way to muddy red soil bordered by lush green grasslands. At first, we saw a few cows and the occasional sheep, but soon it was the order of the day. I had never seen herds and herds of cattle and little boy shepherds. They ran after our cars and happily cheered us on.

I was so lost in thought that it did not occur to me and my cousins that our stomachs were rumbling. It was lunchtime, and there was no sign of a pizza or mac-and-cheese store. John stopped at a popular tourist lunch spot and turned around to ask, "*Na taka ku kula?*"

We shouted a big yes, guessing the obvious question: "Do you want to eat?"

We walked behind the guides down a bushy path into a valley near a river. It was a freshwater trout spot in the middle of the bushes and was built in and around a large Mugumo (sacred fig) tree.

There was a campfire and smoke. Trout was grilling alongside baked potatoes. There were two wooden decks built on large oak trees overlooking the river below with wooden tables and chairs. It was called the Trout Tree Restaurant. This restaurant is located on the Burguret River and is 3km from Nanyuki Civil Airstrip.

There were wooden steps on the large tree going up to the higher-level deck. I was running up the steps with my cousins when something black jumped right out of the hole underneath our feet and ran up the stairs and onto the tree. We all screamed. My heart was pounding, and I was shaking.

"Mommy!" the ASI sisters yelled together.

It was a large mongoose with black and white stripes. It disappeared into the bushes. Some of the tourists who had heard us scream gathered around with their cameras, hoping to catch the excitement on camera.

We settled down and ordered our lunch. While waiting for lunch, we could see trout swimming in the river. Finally, we got our trout and baked potatoes. The waitress warned us to be careful with the monkeys sitting in the trees.

"They could jump onto your table and take the food right off your plate in a split second," explained the head waitress.

While I worked my way through the bones of the fish to get to the meat, I could hear Nana saying, "So, Sarah, how is the taste of the Kenyan trout? Did I not promise you all that this is a once-in-a-lifetime tasting?"

I spoke through a mouthful of fish and potatoes and managed a big, "Yes!"

Daddy added, "This is very fresh but has a distinctly different flavor from what I usually grill in New York." We later took a walk around the property to see the amazing trout ponds.

After our first lunch in the wild, we were back in our open-roofed safari vehicle.

The drive to Ol Pajeta was long and went down rocky, muddy, and bumpy roads. Lush green landscape with deep growth of Acacia trees were the rich character of the terrain. Although the journey was very long, I never felt tired because John kept my mind alert with his thorough knowledge of the land and the African wildlife. He gave us papers and pencils to note names of animals and birds we spotted.

After almost five hours of the dusty ride, we were finally driving through the national park conservancy. I was amazed to see the natives of Ol Pejeta. Both women and men were very tall with absolutely straight backs. They wore traditional red Maasai dresses, called *shuka* in Swahili, which looked like sheets wrapped around the body.

We were told that they use the red color because the lions are scared of red and don't attack people. Women and men were both covered with jewelry and wore headdresses, all made out of multicolored beads and animal skin.

I had waited to see the big game in their natural home. Tall, long-necked giraffes and humongous elephants with long, white tusks like in the *Ice Age* movie were coming to life.

After the drive through the park, we arrived at Sweetwaters Resort, and everyone was a little hot, dusty, and exhausted. We were served with welcoming hot snacks, fresh passion fruit juice, tea, and coffee.

CHAPTER 4
Exploring the Ol Pejeta Sweetwaters Resort and National Park, Day One

July 29, 2019

After the welcoming snacks, we were guided to the reception desk where we met two very pleasant ladies with beaded hair wearing traditional dress. They briefed us about the resort and its highlights. I learnt that it is built in Laikipia County and that Ol-Pejeta is a not-for-profit wildlife conservancy, which provides a sanctuary for animals such as the largest Black Rhino, White Rhino, Chimpanzees and big five game in East Africa. We checked in but dared not to go to our rooms alone. A couple of young porters gave us a short tour of the facility and helped bring our luggage to the room.

I asked them if my room had a hot tub, and they gave me a strange look. I walked along, imagining a huge room with a television and a whirlpool tub. After having walked quite a distance, to my surprise, we were shown into a big, dark, muddy-colored tent made of canvas. The inside was very spacious with beds and a bathroom, but obviously there was no television or whirlpool tub. I then understood why the porter was surprised at my question earlier.

The entrance was nothing but a zipper door. I got nervous when the porter instructed us to keep the door zipped down all the time in order to keep the wild animals from entering, especially the big baboons that were sitting up in large trees around the tent.

This was really tenting in a national park. Next to our tent was a small lake that was visited by waterbucks, gazelles, baboons, and many species of colorful birds. This was something that I had read about in adventure stories, and now I was living it. After a traditional Kikuyu lunch made of *ugali* (Kenyan cornmeal) and *sukuma wiki* (collard greens), we went for a drive into the surrounding national park.

Huge herds of African elephants grazing in a marsh alongside large herds of zebras, gazelles, marabou storks, and giraffes with insanely tall legs and necks made the afternoon scene. The jungle was filled with wildebeests, monkeys, and baboons. It was dusty and hot, but the light breeze helped keep us comfortable. When it started getting dark, we had to return back to our camp. Sounds like the screeching and occasional gibber of monkeys, and chirping of crickets travelled through the evening air.

The dining hall at Sweetwaters was huge and full of tourists. The change in the weather was very pleasant because it was nice and cool by the evening. The cuisine was rich with Swahili dishes like *ugali*, *matokee* (plantains), and *cuckoo paka* (coconut chicken curry). They also served us grilled chicken, steak, grilled long beans, and collard greens. There was light Swahili music and a campfire outside the main hall that made the evening even more beautiful.

We overstayed in the dining area while playing different games. Suddenly, the waiter asked us very politely to leave for our tents. I pictured what it would be like if my whole family walked through a tiny pathway leading to our tents while wildlife lurked throughout the property. To add to my shock, he informed us that there was no electricity in this area except generators that ran for a couple of hours each night and were turned off past midnight.

We quickly got out and found two men waiting for us at the main gate to accompany us to the tent, which was quite a walk. They had lanterns, *pangas* (machetes), and sticks in their hands. One man was in the front and the other behind our group, keeping us safe from wild animal attacks.

My cousins and I were enjoying every bit of this adventure, when, to our amazement, Farina and my mom, who were walking ahead of me, let out a loud scream. Strange, nonhuman shadows with large shining eyes had popped up in the midst of the bushes inside the barbed wire surrounding our tent. Aunt Naz, who was walking behind us, flashed a light onto these shadows, and what we saw was remarkable … These were huge waterbucks. They had two very long ringed horns and large rounded ears. There were white patches above their eyes and around their nose.

Why were they inside the living quarters?

The light from the torch had lit my path well, and here I was running right toward the largest one. The screams of my parents, which I had somehow blocked until that moment, stopped me right in my tracks. The waterbuck and I stared at each other. Time stood still, and then I felt the waterbuck move a little in my direction. The guards were quickly moving in but did not want to scare me or the waterbuck.

The next thing I knew, my feet were on fire and running like the famous Jamaican runner Usain Bolt. In just a few seconds, I found myself being swept up in my daddy's warm embrace. He carried me all the way back to our tent.

Everyone remained silent, and our faces were gray. We entered our tent, and I quickly started zipping down the door. I was now afraid of everything-lions and hippos and all. In my mind, these creatures would enter our tent at night and bring the tent down.

I changed into my pajamas, brushed my teeth, and combed my hair, but I was still numb from the shock. As I slid under the covers, my feet touched something warm, and I shot right out of bed, screaming at the top of my lungs. My whole body was trembling. I imagined this could be a snake or lizard or anything wild.

My parents quickly stripped the covers, and we all had a big laugh of relief. It was a hot-water bottle the staff had provided to keep us warm during the cool nights at Sweetwaters. We all snuggled together in our beds, and my dad calmed me down, assuring me that the security guards on patrol around the property and tents would keep us safe during the night.

CHAPTER 5
Sweetwaters National Park, Day Two

July 30, 2019

The next morning, we started out to the wild very early. We were informed that most of the animals get out for a hunt in the early morning and evening in order to avoid the heat during the day. Lions and cheetahs get exhausted very quickly after their fast chase.

We were in two separate vehicles, and the drivers were communicating with each other through their walkie-talkies. We heard Alfred's voice asking John to turn around to a different location where there was a lion sitting near the bushes in the distance. My heart was racing as we looked at each other, and I held onto Inaya's hand.

My mom asked John if it was safe to go near the lion because the SUV had an open roof and sides.

Mama asked "What if the lion were to jump and take a kid away?"

John replied "Don't worry. The animals are quite far away." He cautioned, "Please remain quiet as we get closer."

The next few miles of driving felt like years until we saw the other vehicle, which had stopped near some tall bushes. Our SUV slowly moved behind the other SUV.

Everyone was looking at one particular bush in the distance, and people had their cameras out. My dad whispered, "Look on the right side of the bush. There is a lion sitting there."

When I looked right, I had to really strain my eyes to see what looked like a brownish *something* far away.

Inaya and I were still holding each other tightly. I had mixed feelings of excitement and fear and now even disappointment. I felt something grab me by the arm.

When I turned around, I was looking into the eyes of a huge brown lion! I was numb, and although I was screaming, no sound could be heard. The lion was pulling me away from everyone I loved, and everything seemed to be dark.

In the far distance, I saw something dark blue at the top and light blue at the bottom. This thing was chasing after the lion and me. It was my dad wearing his dark blue T-shirt and light blue jeans. He was waving a *panga* (machete) at the lion.

The lion dug his sharp claws into my dad's arm, from which drops of dark red blood were oozing…it was both fear and awe to watch the battle between my dad and the lion. In my mind, I could imagine the scene from *The Jungle Book* where *Shere Khan*, the tiger, was fighting with Mowgli.

I felt something tug at my arm and could hear my mom saying, "Did you see the lion?"

I then realized that I was back in my SUV, and all of that had been my imagination. Everyone, including my dad, was still engaged with the lion they had seen in the distance. They had waited for the lion to get up and walk, but I think he had eaten an antelope and was now resting.

John started driving away to explore more of the park. I was happy to be safe with my family and felt relieved. We spotted a big group of giraffes moving from our left side to cross over to the other side.

Apparently, they were going to drink water in a nearby lake. We drove near them and stopped. The giraffes kept walking and crossed the road right in front of us, only a few feet away. Their legs and necks were so tall and heads so high that in order to find their heads I had to look up into the sky as if I were looking up at the clouds.

After a five-hour trip, we went back to camp to eat lunch. Uncle Amir showed me the picture of the lion that folks in our SUV had failed to see. He had managed to capture a close view of the lion on his special camera. It sure looked fierce, and I couldn't help remember the adventure that I had imagined with this lion, just a few hours earlier in the SUV.

We rested and then got ready to go to a very popular tourist spot called Mount Kenya Safari Club. It is situated at the foothills of Mount Kenya, the tallest mountain in Kenya and second tallest mountain in Africa, after Mount Kilimanjaro. The hotel was built in 1955 by Mr. William Holden, a famous American movie actor.

We were greeted by staff. My eyes went straight to their beautiful, locally made flat leather sandals with colorful straps. We walked around the huge property with lush green gardens, a lake, and an exquisitely carved hedge maze. We all entered the maze together but then split into groups and took different directions. However, the ASI group got really lost and started to panic a little.

"I think we should turn right," said Inaya, looking quite pale.

"No, I am pretty sure we should turn left," Ariana suggested in a shaky voice.

I was missing my hero dad and could only say, "Don't worry. We will find a way to get out."

Fear of the baboons that we had seen earlier on the property gripped at our hearts. After a few more tries, we finally made our way out of the hedge maze. The ASI girls were actually the first to come out. When everyone was finally together again and out of this challenge, we all walked to an elaborate seating arrangement for high tea in the gardens.

They had different types of cookies, including my favorite chocolate chip cookies, cakes, tiny sandwiches, and a variety of juices, teas, and coffee. During high tea, we had some unwelcome visitors! Large, hungry marabou storks were lurking around our tables to snatch some sandwiches. Everyone had to keep looking over their shoulders for fear of a close encounter with that very large and strong beak. My dad, Inaya, Ariana, and I tried to later befriend them, but it was not easy.

As we drove back, I decided to do a fun little thing with Inaya. We stuck our heads out and kept shouting, *Jambo (Hello)* to the small children who were waving to us from the roadside as our vehicles sped on. The air brushed our faces, and the sweet smell of the red African soil filled our nostrils. I wondered whether my mom had felt the exact same feelings that I was now experiencing when she had visited the same places in the past.

The next destination after Sweetwaters was Lake Nakuru. This would be a difficult seven-hour raw countryside drive, and although the ASI team would have loved to stay and talk longer after dinner, we all decided to retire for bed early.

CHAPTER 6
Lake Nakuru: Nakuru Sopa Lodge

July 31, 2019

After a quick breakfast the next day, we set out on our drive to Lake Nakuru, one of the largest lakes in the midwestern region of Kenya. In order to get out of Sweetwaters National Park, we had to drive through the park for an hour before hitting a tarmac road. We went through beautiful small towns and made a stopover at a small rest area that had a roadside souvenir shop. The shop was selling beautifully crafted animal and tribesmen figures in a wide range of sizes starting from just a few inches to almost twice my height.

I bought a very colorful beaded bracelet for myself. My parents bought animal figurines and hand-painted handbags.

Before getting back on the road, our drivers had a meeting and came up with the idea of taking a shorter, unpaved, non-tarmac road through the real countryside to get to Lake Nakuru. Their estimate was that it would be a three-hour drive instead of four-and-a-half hours when using the main roads.

Everyone was on the same page, so here we were on an unpaved, muddy road with very few other vehicles. The road was extremely slippery and bumpy. My cousins and I were seated at the back and felt the bumps all the more. At one point, my parents wanted to tell the drivers to turn back. My cousins and I were somehow enjoying this thrilling, bumpy drive, but we were scared too. However, we wanted to see the local villages and people.

It was already past noon when John announced a stopover at a local town situated right on the equator.

As we finished eating our snacks, a young man holding a water bowl approached us and asked us to follow him to see him perform an experiment. The water bowl had a hole right in the middle where he had put his thumb to stop leakage.

He placed the bowl on the flat part of the road about ten feet north of the equator line and put one matchstick in it. The matchstick was steady until he opened the hole in the middle and let the water drain out. The matchstick started in a clockwise movement. Then we moved to a spot that was about ten feet south of the equator line and repeated the same experiment. We were thrilled to see the matchstick moving counterclockwise.

As if this was not enough magic, he urged us to move right on the equator line and repeated this simple experiment again. I gasped as the matchstick stayed steady at one spot. The young man told us that if one's hair grew following a clockwise direction, that person was likely born in the northern hemisphere and if counterclockwise in the southern. The ASI sisters started to check out the pattern of growth on each other and the adults.

When we finished the experiment, we were called inside a small room on one side of the souvenir store and were issued certificates for standing at the equator, obviously after paying 1,000 shillings (8.88 US dollars) for each certificate.

After driving for another two hours through hills, rocky terrain through the Great Rift Valley, we finally saw a glimpse of our lodge, the SOPA Lodge. Before we could say a word, we started feeling huge bumps, especially those of us in the back seat. Sounds like "ouch" were heard from every corner several times. As I looked through the front window, I saw huge boulders and rocks in our way. Even worse, we were going up a mountain. That's where the lodge was. It took us about half-an-hour to finally reach the top.

Upon arrival, we were welcomed by the staff who helped us take our luggage to the reception area. By now, my whole family was exhausted. A nice waitress brought us complimentary juices. I reached for the freshly squeezed passion fruit juice and managed to say, "*Asante sana,*" to her. It was very refreshing.

This time we had to be driven in carts up a tall hill to our rooms. I thought it would be a beaten-down, old hut. The porter was taking our luggage through the door of a large hut.

Aunty Naz remarked "I don't want to sleep in a hut again."

Everyone smiled. No one said a word. We entered the hut to find this lodge had been fashioned to look like huts on the outside, but on the inside, it was pure luxury. There were two large four-poster beds, each with flowy white mosquito nets and a large glass bay window and patio that overlooked the green valley and Lake Nakuru.

The sun was still up, and there was a short drizzle. We took some pictures. After a quick wash and change of clothes, we were picked up in carts to go to the dining room for a bite. Soon we were back in our vehicles and heading down to Lake Nakuru to see the flamingos. Before we reached the water, we saw herds of antelopes and buffalos. We were closer to the water and could see a pink and white layer of flamingos floating in the water.

Ariana mentioned, "We are supposed to see other species including herons, storks, pelicans, and other wading birds."

My dad answered "That is correct. There are over 1 million lesser and greater flamingos on this lake, if only we could get closer."

The weather in these parts is unpredictable and can change before you can count to ten, and true enough, it started to pour. Within the next few minutes, it was teeming. Potholes started to fill up and flood.

My dad nervously remarked, "John, I hope we don't get stuck."

John, our driver, was nervous too and was talking on the walkie-talkie with Alfred. Both drivers decided that we should get out of there as soon as possible. They feared that the SUV would sink into the mud and get stuck. The engine kept on going *vroom, vroom* while John was pushing the accelerator, but the SUV sank deeper into the clay.

I thought to myself, *What if we got stuck here? There would be no one to help us.*

We were sure stuck! The mud was like clay, which when mixed with water makes a very thick and sticky mixture. Everyone was holding their breath, and my mom clenched her hands.

"Guys, it's getting dark, it's wet, and this is jungle … What are we going to do?" she exclaimed.

Farina countered that with a positive comment. "John won't let that happen. He has a lot of experience."

Of course, I thought to myself and felt reassured.

It was a miracle that when John pushed the accelerator hard a few more times, the car started to move again. Finally, we could get going on our journey. Everyone let out a big sigh of relief and thanked John profusely.

A divine Mediterranean and Swahili dinner awaited us in the luxurious glass-paneled dining room. The food was out-of-this-world. There were many stations with varieties of vegetables cooked in different ways, dried fruits, cheese, and freshly baked breads. We also got a hibachi-like feel at one station because a well-trained chef was cooking our meats right in front of us.

But something did not seem right. I felt that one food was missing and could not quite remember what. Then I remembered it was *ugali*. This is a type of maize flour porridge, which is a staple diet of Africans. My mom made a special request for Ugali, and the waiter immediately brought a platter of Ugali right to our table. My cousins and I could not stop talking about the adventures we had that day.

CHAPTER 7
Maasai Mara, Day One: Mara River Camp Lodge

August 1, 2019

I could not believe how fast the days were speeding by. It was already August 1st, and we were on our way to the world-renowned Maasai Mara National Reserve. For months prior to our trip to Kenya, Dad, Nana, Uncle Amir, and Nabeel had spent endless hours of internet searches and phone calls with their tour guides to come up with a booking at the Mara River Camp Resort in Mara.

We arrived at the resort in late afternoon after a ride through wide valleys and escarpments. This lodge is located on the banks of the famous Mara River in the middle of a jungle with very tall Acacia trees and bushes. The word Mara means spotted land. It was coined to describe a bird's eye view of a land which is dotted with Acacia trees. These trees bear thorns and are food for the herbivore animals of the Mara. Acacia trees tend to thrive in the semi-arid climate of the Mara and it's heavy clay soil. Mara River is huge and a home to hippos and crocodiles.

The tent in Mara was completely made from canvas and wood. The windows were netted and had a flap of canvas that could be unzipped for a covering. There was a small stone patio outside with a fireplace overlooking the river. One had to walk through this wild jungle in order to get to the dining area.

Everyone showered and dressed nicely for dinner. The chef was a very sweet man and took special care to make us feel at home. My Aunt Naz, who is both charming herself and friendly, spoke in Swahili with him, and we were soon served special treats like samosas and steak that were not even on the menu that night.

Inaya, Ariana, and I played dominoes while the adults chatted by the cozy fireplace and sipped coffee. The walk back to the tents was a little nerve-racking, as we had heard stories about close encounters between guests and hippos. I could hear them as they grunted in the river very close to the tents. The shadows danced around in the dim lights, running our imagination wild, as we nervously giggled and ran to our tents. I made sure that

the zipper was all the way down. My mother is scared of snakes, and she was not comfortable at all about the small space left even when all three of the zippers were closed. I knew she would not sleep.

A strange wheezing sound woke us up in the middle of the night. My dad shone his flashlight through the netted window and whispered for us to come near the window. I was scared and was holding my breath and my mom's arm tightly. There was a huge hippo next to our tent looking in our direction, breathing and puffing loudly with intermittent grunts. It had come out of the river to walk around and graze on the banks. It did not move or threaten us, but I could not fall asleep right away and kept thinking about the hippo.

CHAPTER 8
Maasai Mara, Day Two: Picnic in the Wild

August 2, 2019

It was early dawn and still quite dark despite the dim camp lights. My family looked like shadows carefully making their way toward the dining room to meet Alfred and John for an early breakfast before the game drive in the Mara.

I was tired from the events of the night and hungry. However, a strange and gripping excitement was growing in my heart, and it did not matter anymore that I had not slept enough.

My mother had shared her experiences of having watched a live hunt by a lion in the Mara, or an actual kill as she had put it.

Now it was my turn, and although I felt brave enough, I was also a little scared. Since Maasai Mara is famous for the big five: elephant, lion leopard, rhino and Cape buffalo, the ASI sisters were hoping to see all of them here.

Nana gently smiled as he said, "Whoever can spot all of the big five will earn a treat from me."

"How much? How much?" cried out all three of the ASI.

We had almost empty piggy banks awaiting us in New York, and we assumed the reward would be dollars.

My dad jested, saying, "I know what Nana's treat will be. He will sing us all a favorite Elvis number!"

Now, the ASI sisters thought that sure would be a lovely treat, although getting a few bucks always felt so good.

At the front desk, baskets with sandwiches, fruit, and drinks for the picnic lunch were neatly stacked for us to pick up on our way out. Everyone except my mother ate fast, almost as if they inhaled their breakfast and made a dash to find favorite spots in each of the two jeeps.

Mama remarked, "Guys, please relax and enjoy every moment … I am taking my time to do justice to these delicious *mandazis* (coconut donuts) and my coffee. Save a seat for me."

As the jeeps drove off into the expanse of the Mara Reserve, clouds of dust began to gather and follow us.

A herd of impalas walked right in front of us. Their ambling indicated that there was no big game hanging around. It amazed me to see how these animals had grown used to seeing jeeps and humans.

These herds were a local *park compass,* I thought to myself, and surely John and Alfred turned their cars around to follow an alternative route hoping to find some big game.

Aunty Naz joked, "At least here the impalas have some peace without the big cats!"

Farina chuckled, "I am happy for the impalas but sad that the girls may not see the big five!"

A herd of elephants had not seen us coming. They were either ignoring our presence or too busy enjoying their morning mud bath. We stood still but did not dare get out of the vehicle. Uncle Amir and my dad took pictures.

It was scary yet exciting to see elephants at such a close range. With their front legs, they removed the soil around the grass to weaken the support and then snatched the grass with their trunks before shoving it into their mouths. This reminded me of farmers harvesting their crops in harmony.

Daddy's eyes shone as I shared my thoughts. He smiled and patted my back as he said, "That is a smart analogy … It's quite accurate, and now you have seen the first of the big five in the Mara."

The drivers were more interested in the big cats. John had mentioned how most tourists would get disappointed if they did not spot either a lion, a cheetah, or a leopard. We drove for miles without realizing that the sun had long come up and there was much activity in the park. John and Alfred lined up their jeeps and headed in the same direction. They followed vultures sitting on trees next to a small river. Soon, a few hyenas appeared close to the jeeps. They had blood on their faces and were circling around the jeep.

A chill ran down my back, and Inaya was startled. "Sarah, look … These hyenas are too scary," she cried.

Hyenas can be both predators and feast on animals that have been killed by other animals, such as lions. As we moved closer, we saw a few more hyenas eating a huge buffalo that had apparently been killed by lions earlier in the day. We quickly drove to the scene, and John stopped the SUV just a few feet from the buffalo.

The hyenas looked at us with their faces full of blood and a menacing look in their eyes. My uncle Amir stood up in the open jeep with his camera and positioned himself for the best shot. "Everyone, whenever possible, please try to glance into the camera … I am shooting," he remarked.

While we were watching this incredible scene that could have been from a National Geographic documentary, the hyenas started backing off from the carcass. We turned to the right and saw a large pride of lions approaching the dead buffalo. As they came closer, they moved faster and then ran after the hyenas and chased them away from their kill. They had five cute little lion cubs with them. The cubs were playing around while two big cats were chasing the hyenas away and guarding the pride.

We took a lot of photos. The female lions are the hunters, while the males watch the pride. We had finally seen a lion in the Mara! It took about an hour for the dramatic scene to be over. Life in the wild was very hard to understand. What was right, and what was wrong? Whose side would I take? I was drained, and the drive to the riverbank for a picnic in the jungle was a welcome one.

This is the home of the hippos and crocodiles. There, they lie almost lifeless, like rocks, basking in the sun near the riverbank. Both drivers urged us to come out of the jeeps, and I sank deeper into my seat. *This was not happening*, I thought.

My cousins and I quietly obeyed the orders and stepped onto the rich red soil of the Mara. I was numb with fear and was standing in the middle of a national park that was home to many species of wild animals, including venomous snakes. We constantly felt the urge to turn back and look around for any unwelcome guests.

Our dinner table and chairs were the nearby rocks which felt quite comfortable as we tucked into our individual picnic lunch boxes. Because there were no bathrooms around, the next challenge for many of us was to answer the call of nature behind nearby bushes. I could not help but remember John's words about the sneaky leopards that hide low within the bushes and how they could silently creep up on their prey. Some of us took shelter behind larger bushes, while Uncle Amir, Dad, and Nana watched out for any wildlife. That was my scariest bathroom experience ever, but it is one I will never forget.

After tea and snacks, we got back into the jeeps for the next adventure in the Mara. The afternoon was spent looking for the other two big cats: leopards and cheetahs. My mother had shared her experience when she and Nana had last visited the Mara. I could clearly imagine her words describing cheetah cubs hanging down from the Acacia trees like fruits and playfully rolling from side to side as they fell … hmmm, how exciting that must have been!

The two jeeps decided to go separate ways and alert the other on the radio when either a leopard or cheetah was seen. While we were lucky to see a lonely cheetah wandering around in the high grass, Alfred's SUV had no such luck. They feasted their eyes on the numerous zebras, wildebeests, impalas, buffalos, and a few species of birds that many may never see in their lives. This was yet another memorable experience driving through the Mara even though we had not completed seeing the list of the big five.

That night we all had a very short and interrupted sleep because we had to be up before dawn to go for one of the most unusual flying experiences. It's something that has always been described as a truly exotic Safari experience-the balloon safari in the Mara. This adventure was planned to make up for the missed opportunity when we had visited Turkey the previous year.

A balloon safari in Cappadocia was the most coveted feat for tourists traveling to Turkey and touted for its breathtaking views, but due to bad weather we had missed it during our 2018 trip to Turkey. So, when my dad and family booked the balloon ride in Maasai Mara, my excitement knew no bounds. The trip thus far had been so lovely, but I did miss my sleep and my bed in New York and tonight was not going to be any different.

CHAPTER 9
Maasai Mara, Day Three: Balloon Ride

August 3, 2019

It was just 5 am when we were picked up by a driver in a vehicle that looked and felt like an armored tank. The jeep crawled through the rocky road in the darkness of this early morning. From very far, we could see the shimmering lights of the launchpad on top of a hill.

The road was bumpy with boulders. I tried to stay steady in my seat but slammed my head into the rollbar above my seat. I cried out, tears welling in my eyes. My dad, my hero, was right there again to console me, and I could feel his hug grow tighter around my arms as his soothing voice whispered into my ear, "Where is my strong girl? I know it hurts now, but thank God it's a minor bruise. As soon as you fly over Mara, you will forget this pain, I promise."

When we reached the launchpad, there was a line of people waiting to get into the camp. After checking us in, we were guided to an open waiting area with some coffee and tea. Ariana and Inaya gathered around me like a doctor and nurse to look at my head, and we were all relieved that the injury was minor.

"Will the patient live?" joked Nana, looking at Inaya who nodded her very cute, curly head.

It took around forty minutes before we were taken to the hot-air balloon boarding site, but it had seemed like hours to me, and my head was a little sore. Now we were standing next to our first hot-air balloon basket. The pilot demonstrated how one was to get into the basket and then made us sign some more documents.

I found myself being helped into a tilted basket linked to a giant deflated balloon. The pilot lit a fire under the balloon, which then started to expand, and the basket straightened up. It felt very hot because the fire was right over our heads. I laughed to see all the adults secure their hats as if to protect the tops of their heads from the burning fire above.

Before long, we took off and found ourselves floating over the grasslands of Maasai Mara. The noise of the engine caused an angry elephant a few feet below us to send out a warning trumpet as if to say, "Do not disturb!"

I agreed with the elephant because my parents create a very peaceful ambience during mealtimes, especially breakfast. On the other hand, it was so much fun! I felt like I was flying like a bird. In the beginning of the flight, the balloon was flying very low and touched some treetops that felt like a slap on the bucket.

The vast landscape just opened up before our eyes, and although we did not see any animals other than impalas and waterbucks, the view itself was magnificent. We continued to fly for about a half-hour more when the pilot announced that the landing would be rough because of the wind. The landing came too soon, and he was not joking!

Our basket tilted and dragged for a bit before it hit the ground hard with a thud, sending shrieks of discomfort from all of us. It lifted again, and after it was in the air for a few seconds, it hit the ground hard again. This time, I felt my neck would break. This process repeated itself a few more times with several hits and thuds and lifts before it came to a halt.

We had landed in the middle of nowhere in tall grass with a few scattered bushes around which anything could be hiding, especially a snake. My imagination was running wild, and I was clutching onto whatever I could grab. No one waited to hear the pilot's instructions. We all jumped out of the basket and ran for our lives through long grass that came up to my neck in order to reach the waiting SUVs. Farina and my mom are both terrified of snakes, so they ran the fastest.

We were driven to an open space for breakfast right in the wild! There were guards protecting the breakfast area. Fresh cut fruit with American heart-shaped waffles, hot scrambled eggs, toast, muffins, freshly squeezed orange juice, and coffee elegantly laid out in white tents awaited us. In addition, we were honored with certificates for having successfully completed the balloon ride. This was my second Kenyan certificate of accomplishment, and the ASI sisters felt very important.

Around 9 am we were done with the balloon ride and started the lion and leopard hunt in the vast savannas of Maasai Mara. As always, we were in two different vehicles, and the drivers were communicating with each other through their walkie-talkies. We heard Alfred's voice over the walkie-talkie. "*Bwana pindua gari.*" He was telling John to turn the car around. He had spotted something in a different location.

My heart was racing as we looked at each other, and I held onto Inaya's hand. Mama asked John if it was safe to go near lions or the bigger cats given that the SUV had an open top and sides. This would not be the first time she had posed this question.

We all smiled knowingly, but I could not help echo her fears. *What if the lion were to jump and hurt someone?* I thought.

John told us not to worry but to remain quiet. The next few miles of driving felt like years until we saw a few vehicles parked near a small rock surrounded by bushes. Our SUV slowly moved next to the other SUV.

Everyone was looking at one particular bush, and people had their cameras out. My dad whispered, "Look on the right side of the bush. There is a lion sitting there with little cubs."

When I looked to the right, I saw a big brown lion and a few lionesses sitting right in front of me. This felt very close, yet I was no longer afraid. It looked like the lion family was resting, but the cubs were playing around. Someone whispered, "Look to the left," and we all turned to see a smaller bush next to which a lioness was sitting on a rock all alone. It seemed that she was keenly looking out for any danger to the cubs on the opposite side. Her sharp brown eyes were alert, and I could not help but stare.

Three more SUVs had arrived at the scene and were also lined up surrounding the bush. One of the more enthusiastic drivers pushed his SUV closer to the bush to impress his tourists and did not realize that he would get stuck in the rocks. After a few minutes, we could hear his engine go *vroom, vroom*. This was a reminder of what had happened to our vehicle at Lake Nakuru. He backed his vehicle, but the car was stuck between big rocks. He tried to maneuver the SUV out, but it would not budge.

The quiet air around was now filled with engine noise, and we were all concerned. He talked to another driver apparently for help to tow his car. Both the drivers came out of their SUVs holding a rope. A red flag showed up in my head because my parents had cautioned me to never ever get outside any vehicle in the middle of the jungle on the trip.

"That would mean you are inviting the animals to come close and even attack you," my dad had explained.

The drivers seemed to be oblivious to this warning and were outside their vehicles, trying to tie the rope to some hooks in both vehicles in order to help pull out the stranded vehicle. Everyone felt afraid for the drivers. This was too close a range between the drivers and the lions, especially their little cubs.

Uncle Amir and Nana could not hold back their concern for the drivers and said, "The lionesses may feel threatened for their cubs and could attack the drivers." They had hardly finished saying this when the lone lioness on the left side moved a little, as if to stand up. She seemed alert and was staring at the men at work outside their vehicles. Suddenly, she raised her head and positioned her body, ready to charge!

My dad yelled, "She is coming!"

We all turned to our left, drawn by the growls from the lioness as she first moved swiftly and then sprinted toward the drivers. Everyone was nervous, and people from all the SUVs were calling out to the drivers to get back in their open-roofed vehicles. Most of the SUV vehicles had only an open roof but side doors. The drivers finished tying the needed knots just in time to jump back in their vehicles before the lioness could get close enough. The lioness stopped her sprint abruptly next to the SUV, as if to signal that the threat to her cubs had subsided. She stared at the men who now sat safely in their SUV and then she moved away.

We all were tense and I felt like my heart would come out of my chest. Everyone was clutching their hands in a state of fear and shock. What a close encounter!

The lioness proudly moved right in front of our vehicles and slowly joined the rest of the pride. I know she too was relieved that any threat to her cubs had passed. I will never forget this episode! Everyone in my car could only talk about the lioness for the rest of the journey.

John told us stories of his own close encounters with lions. He also informed us that Alfred had actually hunted and killed a lion as a teenager, which was a tradition of his Maasai heritage. This made me respect both John and Alfred even more, and I knew they would protect us.

John slowed his car and turned around, saying, "Now your big five list is getting closer to being complete. Look what is walking toward us."

A lone cheetah was walking along the dry roadside as if looking to hunt. He ignored us and carried on walking into the tall savanna grass of the Mara. It was a very elegant looking animal, and I recalled that it was a fast runner with a speed of almost sixty miles an hour.

Mama pulled out an Oreo cookie bag, and we all helped ourselves. The drivers were very motivated to keep looking for a leopard in the trees. However we were not lucky enough to see one.

That evening back at the resort, we were entertained by the Maasai dancers during dinner. I wanted to jump as high as they could, but it was very difficult. I have this on my to-do list, and one day I hope to be able to also jump as high.

CHAPTER 10
Back to Nairobi After Mara: Meeting the Family

August 4, 2019

We enjoyed the long drive back to Nairobi from the Mara. John kept us engaged with his thorough commentary about African wildlife, politics, traditions, and economy. My dad was hungry and remembered that charcoal-grilled Kenyan corn is very popular. John knew exactly the right spot for the best corn and drove us to a small township close by.

Our vehicles had not come to a complete stop, when a crowd of young boys encircled our SUVs from all sides. They were holding out freshly grilled corn on the cob and tried to sell it to us by pushing it through any open window right in front of our faces. My window was half closed, but five very bright-eyed young children were pushing it down and actually managed to open it and pushed their corn right in. One of the vendors accidentally hit my dad's cheek with the hot corn. We all had a great laugh and thoroughly relished the corn as a treat.

The first leg of our trip was almost done, but there was one more important detail. It was meeting the family in Nairobi. This would be a first meeting between the ASI and most of the family in Kenya, except Aunty Pini.

My family had arranged a luncheon for everyone at a restaurant called Anghiti (Charcoal Grill). The restaurant was soon flocked with people of all ages, even five-month-old babies. All these faces seemed so strange, yet there was a connection.

This was my mother's family: aunts, uncles, cousins, nieces, nephews, and their little ones. It felt powerful to know that so many people somewhere in the world belonged together. They hugged, kissed, and cried and soon became comfortable talking with each other. There were also some speeches from my aunt, Nana, and Mama, who all are really good at public speaking.

Aunty Naz, a seasoned toastmaster, was at her best that evening. This was her stage, and she sent a message of love, loud and clear, to everyone. My Uncle Nana, another accomplished toastmaster, extended a warm welcome and sent out a beautiful message. Many family members had tears in their eyes and a broad smile on their lips after he spoke.

The ASI sisters felt very important because everyone kept hugging and praising us. We were having a lot of fun, although the food was not that tasty, I must add. I made strong bonds with my mother's cousins, Uncle Zaffer, Aunty Shamim, Aunty Naseem, and Uncle Zaffer's wife Aunty Dee. The ASI felt a strong affinity to Aunty Pini.

Aunty Pini, besides being a wonderful cook and hostess, has a huge heart. Later that evening she extended the hospitality of her home to everyone, serving yet another divine dinner in Nairobi.

This was a very special evening where both Nana and I were able to give everyone a taste of our singing. Inaya and Mama sang too. Singing is a big hobby in our family. Nana sings like Elvis Presley, and both him and my mom are members of singing clubs that perform at different events. I want to be a singer when I grow up, among so many other things.

That night I took to the stage, grabbed the microphone, and rocked the stage when I sang "A Million Dreams." Next, Inaya sang her favorite number, "Fight Song," and everyone clapped for us. In a short time, I had so many fans, especially my cousins, who all took selfies with us.

That evening when we returned to IBIS Styles Hotel, Farina's brother Nabeel and his wife, Rimma, had also arrived from New York to join us on the second leg of our trip. They were waiting for us in the lobby. Nabeel is our best buddy and holds a very special place in my heart. I was thrilled to see him. We all jumped onto his neck and just could not get enough of him.

CHAPTER 11
Off to Amboseli National Park, Day One

August 5, 2019

Amboseli National Park is 150 miles south of Nairobi, right next to Mount Kilimanjaro, Africa's highest peak. The name *Amboseli* comes from a Maasai word that means "salty dust." The animal that best defines this park is the great big elephant with the longest tusks ever. I had heard that the animals of this park are *designer* animals because of their unique features.

After a long day's drive to Amboseli, we were held up at the gate of the national park due to a long line of tourists before us. We kept hoping to get in that day, but after two hours of waiting in the hot and dusty SUVs, we saw John and Alfred return with the news that we were too late to enter the park and would have to come back the next day.

This was a big disappointment, and we were driven to our lodge, which also happened to be a branch of the Sopa Lodge. A very tall Maasai man was standing at the reception desk. My guess was that he was at least seven feet tall. We were assigned huts, and ours was number 60.

A bodyguard had to accompany us to and from the huts because the property was not fenced, enabling wild animals to walk back and forth freely. The huts at Sopa Lodge looked different from those we had stayed in at Lake Nakuru. These looked more like mud huts from the outside but were squeaky clean and comfortable and had all the necessary amenities inside. Many tourists would love to spend a night there because the lodge gives you a more natural feel of being in the national park.

CHAPTER 12
Amboseli, Day Two

August 6, 2019

As had become our routine, we were up early and very eager to see what Amboseli would hold in store for us. I was curious why the term *designer* was used for animals. Mama refrained from telling me the answer because she wanted me to find the answer myself.

Excited, we entered the park after almost an hour-long drive down a very dusty road. On the way to the park, we saw the magical sunrise hitting the peak of Mount Kilimanjaro and took pictures. Soon we saw herds of large black elephants with very long white tusks going for breakfast in the marsh, which was also full of green grass. It was a sight to watch them feed and bathe in the mud.

To our disappointment, we did not see the world's largest elephant, which was reported to live in this park. However, we saw a lot of impalas, waterbucks, and other animals, such as Egyptian ducks, a variety of colorful birds, and very large ostriches. John explained that the black ostriches were male, while the brown ones were female. There were different types of zebras, some of which looked shorter and browner in color. I could now see why the term *designer* had been coined by tourists for these animals.

Soon we came across a freshly killed zebra with a lioness sitting right next to it. Her face was full of blood, and she was panting. By now, my list of animals had grown quite long. I could not help feel some despair for the zebra and yet the lioness was also justified in her actions. Perhaps *I would understand things better* when I was older, I thought to myself.

The adults were sharing their past experiences in Amboseli, and it seemed that there was a favorite tea spot called the Serena Lodge.

The last time Mama and Uncle Hamid had visited Amboseli was in 2006. Uncle Hamid recalled, how back in the day this lodge was not only elegantly decorated in bright colors and shapes of Maasai warriors, but was also famous for its cuisine. It was decided that our tea break would be at the Serena Lodge.

The Serena Lodge is famous for its awe-inspiring view of Mount Kilimanjaro and is situated within a grove of Acacia trees. At the Serena Lodge, we were seated out on the porch overlooking the vast green savanna, rich with animals. The chairs at the lodge were so comfortable that after the long ride in the open-sided vehicles, it felt like I was floating on a cloud.

Afternoon tea was served by very polite and pleasant waiters. The high tea consisted of delicious chicken wings, sandwiches, cakes, cookies, and tea served in silver pots. I had ordered chocolate ice cream, and its taste was heavenly, unlike any ice cream I had tried before. It tasted better than the gelatos in Italy. It was a beautiful, serene afternoon, and we all lazed leisurely in this heavenly place.

Tea had just been served, and then someone very small and brown jumped right onto one of our tables, grabbed the small packets of sugar from the trays, and set to work. It was a vervet monkey and I was dumbfounded and scared to see it at such close quarters. Everyone was motionless.

My dad grabbed my cousin Inaya's doll to shoo off the unwelcome visitor, but we were all shocked to see the monkey hold his ground by grunting, squeaking, and even showing a set of brown teeth. My dad imitated the monkey, which annoyed the monkey even more. Then the animal cut open the pouches of sugar, drained the contents into its mouth, and discarded the papers. In so doing, he spilt the milk and kept going for more sugar. Meanwhile, his demeanor had also changed to more aggressive should anyone try again to either take his sugar away from him or him away from this sweet treasure. The show of teeth was now more intermittent, as if to say, "I am in control here!" Even *The Jungle Book* could not have captured these moments better.

I was impressed with the smart technique to discard the paper. The animal had probably acquired the technique through a long time of mere observation of tourists who had sat at this location before us. Soon the gardens were flocked with more monkeys, all jumping from the trees to the wooden fence and onto the tables.

My uncle managed to capture a few more good shots of this most unforgettable experience with his favorite camera. The guards and waiters all shouted, "*Nugu,*" as they watched the scene. They brought out red scarves and shooed the monkey away. Later, I discovered that *nugu* was a nickname for the monkey.

That was our last night in the wild and also the last national park on our journey. Somehow, the ASI were left wanting more of this beautiful experience.

CHAPTER 13
Mombasa, Day One

August 7, 2019

The last leg of our Kenyan trip was to visit Mombasa. The drive from Amboseli to Mombasa was six hours. However, the route that our drivers took was very scenic, and they drove us down unpaved inner countryside roads that went from hills to valleys. On the way, we saw lush green corn fields and different species of Acacia trees and bushes. The small yellow and white flowers on some of these trees accentuated the skyline creating intricate arcades. Many local people seemed to be on foot and often waved to us as we drove by. They seemed very happy and so did I.

To top it off, it was Ariana's birthday, and we all wanted to surprise her later that evening. Inaya and I secretly planned the surprise with my dad. Ariana seemed happy anyway to celebrate her birthday in this very special country, which happened to be her mother, Farina's, birthplace too. The smile on her face that day was especially bright and big.

My mom and Nana kept us entertained with their sweet singing and Nana's guitar. We all got a turn to join in with the singing, and John enjoyed the free show that we put on for him. He kept remarking, "*Mzuri sana!*" which in Swahili means, "Very good!"

As we got closer to Mombasa, there were very large baobab trees with thick trunks as well as palm trees. It reminded me of Florida. Mombasa is a coastal beach city along the Indian Ocean. It is also the second largest city on the east coast of Kenya, which is famous for its soft white sand beaches and luxurious resorts.

My dad remarked, "The culture in Mombasa is a blend of three cultures comprising Swahili, Arabian, and Indian. You will see this reflected in the food, architecture, religions, and people." He added: "Quite the melting pot!"

Aunty Naz said, "It also has historical areas such as the old town, which I hope we can visit when we meet my Uncle Chacha."

It was interesting to see how the city was done in blue and white colors, reminding me of parts of the older towns in Dubai, which is another favorite vacation spot of mine. The buildings were mostly painted white and blue, some almost rustic from the years of wear and tear.

We were booked to stay on the south coast at the Diani Baobab Beach Resort.

Water has a special attraction for me, and I love to be in the pool or at the beach whenever possible. My two cousins and I were extremely excited to finally see the Baobab Hotel. We were surprised to see the endless stretch of white sand and clear blue water like we had never seen before. We looked over the sites through the large glass windows and doors of this luxurious resort's main lobby. After we had been assigned our rooms, we decided to tour the property.

The palm trees were swaying from side to side because of the strong afternoon wind and rain. The gardens around the hotel had many huge boulders. At the seafront, some young, barefooted Swahili boys were selling coconuts and shouted, "*Madaf*," the Swahili word for coconut. Some of the tourists were stopping during their beach walk to buy the *madafs* from these young hawkers.

The sea was crowded with people on Jet Skis, boats, and swimmers. There was a little drizzle, but it was humid yet not unpleasantly warm. My mom, Farina, and I decided to take a walk along the shoreline. The feel of my feet digging into the soft white sand reminded me of my silk quilt back in New York. I would run a little ahead and then run back to my mom, and we would laugh. Her face was relaxed as the soft breeze brushed back her long black hair. She reminded me of Princess Jasmine from *Aladdin*, although her hair is almost as long as Rapunzel's but not blonde. Her eyes were semi-closed to keep the glare of the sun out.

I raised my face up to smile at Mama who had gently slipped her hand into mine. Our eyes met, and I told her how much I loved her favorite beach spot in the world. Farina was also smiling, and she reminded me of Anna from *Frozen*. She and Mama are like blood sisters and happy to hang out together whenever they get a chance. Farina is a very gentle, loving, and kind person who shares a very close relationship with me and Mama. She looked more relaxed too, and I knew in that moment how much I also loved her.

Ariana had joined us slowly, and we both playfully started a sand ball battle. We walked for quite a while. No one wanted to stop, but I was missing my dad.

That evening we enjoyed a dinner in the hotel in their main dining room, which was massive and served a huge assortment of special dishes, mocktails and ice creams. I wanted to try anything that was authentic Mombasa food, and my dad was going to guide me to that particular corner of the buffet. He informed me that due to the Arabic influence, the local Swahili people had adopted a lot of recipes that use fresh coconut milk.

My dad had planned a surprise for Ariana and arranged to have the waiters sing to her after dinner. People in Diani Beach seemed so polite, friendly, and eager to help.

I thought to myself, *How sweet it would be to live here and swim in this clear blue ocean every day! In fact, how about if we could just live at the Diani Baobab Beach Resort and also swim in the two giant pools that were on different levels of the hotel grounds.* My imagination was traveling again, but I was brought back by the sound of clapping and singing.

Everyone at my table was singing "Happy Birthday" to Ariana along with the hotel waiters, and I joined in cheering them along. You should have seen Ariana's jaw drop as my dad put a cake in front of her, lit with candles and the singing waiters. She looked like a princess as the candlelight struck her face and hair, giving her a happy glow.

Ariana was so grateful and remarked "This was the highlight of the day and one of the best birthday treats I could have asked for."

The walk back to the rooms was an interesting one since we would have to be careful of baboons that were waiting on the sidewalks as if to greet us. They lived in the trees surrounding the entire property. We were cautioned not to feed or engage them because they could attack unknowingly.

Our rooms were on the third floor, and the ASI sisters silently rejoiced that we would finally be sleeping in a proper room and not a hut. Each of our rooms had a large balcony overlooking one of the two swimming pools, and it would have been nice to let some breeze in from the balcony. The hotel administration, however, had warned us to keep the balcony doors locked because the monkeys had mastered the art of opening unlocked balcony doors. Tourists had lost valuable items.

I cherished sleeping in this large four-poster bed with a huge mosquito net flowing over it. That night I dreamt of swimming in the sea and meeting a huge jellyfish. My mom had told me stories of how she and her brother had sometimes been stung by jellyfish when they had swum out far into the sea.

CHAPTER 14
Mombasa, Day Two

August 8, 2019

Breakfast was a treat, and I could smell the ocean and feel the breeze as I happily tucked into my chocolate donuts while others awaited to be served their individual entrees. Everyone bonded and talked over a lengthy meal that first morning. Some monkeys had also started their little drama, with tourists who were sitting too close to the windows. Time was very important, and we wanted to soak everything in. I took charge and announced that we should visit the beach after breakfast. We all changed into swimsuits and headed out to the beach.

My dad, Nabeel, and Uncle Amir had an amazing surprise planned for us. Our first activity on the beach was going to be snorkeling. We were taken by a glass-bottomed boat out to sea by the hired boatmen who seemed to be both excellent boatmen and swimmers.

We rode in the boat for quite a distance into the sea and watched colorful sea life through the glass floor. At one point, the boatmen parked and stepped into the sea to bring out various species of sea animals, including varieties of starfish, sea urchins, and crabs for us to touch. We all dared to hold them, and I even let one crawl all over me! I knew then that I had reached hero status through this small feat by the admiring looks of everyone around me. As the boat drew close to the coral reef, we saw long white saltwater snakes with black stripes swimming around the weeds. This sent shivers down my spine, and both my cousin and mom were horrified. Soon the boatmen stopped again for us to get out and start snorkeling. With mixed feelings of excitement and fear everyone got down from the boat into the sea.

I was surprised that although we had come out very far from the beach, the sea here had some really shallow and some very deep spots due to the coral reef. One could be walking on the coral and the next step would lead to a drop into the very deep sea. I was snorkeling among weeds, small barracudas, and lots of colorful fish. It was a relief that I did not see the striped snakes. The ASI sisters were not happy when the boatmen called us to return to the boats for the return journey.

Everyone, except the ASI sisters, was tired and it was getting close to snack time. After the beach fun, the ASI sisters decided to try out the hotel's two large swimming pools, which were located on different levels. We dove and raced with one another.

That night we would eat at the second dining hall of the property, which was located a little farther on the opposite side. Dinner was slightly different from the first night with more international varieties. We helped ourselves to a mixture of plantains, *kuku paka* (coconut curried chicken) and coconut rice, steak, grilled vegetables, and fish. Dessert was a delicious combination of Swahili coconut patties, puddings, local ice creams, and a big tray of mixed fresh fruit. I had yet to taste such delicious, fresh passion fruit and honey-sweet pineapples. To top it all off, we had a go at the fresh *madafs*.

Nana made a decision for all of us to have a lazy evening at the hotel after dinner because the next couple of days were going to be jam-packed with surprises and exciting events. Each night at the hotel, there was a live show put together by local dancers, actors, and musicians. This was such a treat. That night I was invited onto the stage to join in with the singers, and I found myself singing "We Are the World" with the singers on stage. Everyone was clapping.

I did not want to return to my room, but it was getting late. Reluctantly, we all left the show with an amazing memory of our second night in Mombasa.

CHAPTER 15
Mombasa, Day Three

August 9, 2019

It was five o'clock in the morning, and I dared to nudge my dad who was still snoring. "Daddy, please wake up, and let's go for a dip in the ocean before the sun gets too hot."

Within a few minutes, we were both heading off to the beach. The wide expanse of water and the morning rays of sun were a sight to see. We both stood a little to soak it all in and then gingerly put our feet into the water, which felt neither hot nor cold. As I practiced my strokes parallel to my dad, it was almost effortless, and the deep, clear water was like a mattress that I could have slept upon. Now I understood what Grandma had meant about the magic of the ocean.

As we swam, I would go underwater and open my eyes to see any sea life. Aside from some small fish and weeds, I did not see anything. The water was still. Nana and Nabeel had often talked about low and high tides and their connection with the moon. It was all making better sense now.

"Ouch," my dad cried out because something sharp had stung him. I saw him pull off his chest what looked like a long thread. His skin was red, but he seemed otherwise fine.

"Jellyfish sting," he explained, trying a forced smile.

Mama had mentioned similar encounters while swimming in either the early morning or late evening in Mombasa. I thought it was brave of my dad not to cry. When we headed back to take a dip in the pool before breakfast, I was surprised to see the pool already getting crowded with boys and girls of my age.

Aunty Naz reminded us that we had hairdo appointments at the beach. I remembered having seen small kiosks on the sandy beach just a few feet away from the stone steps leading back into the hotel. The ASI team had been curious to see a group of African women sitting right on the sand braiding and beading the hair of some tourist women. Their very simple kiosks had lit up with color as numerous African T-shirts (also known as *kengas*), skirts, scarves, hats, and sheets (*shukas*) swayed in the wind as they hung in neat rows, ready for sale.

As we entered their tent-like beachside salon, they had us sit on small ottomans on the sand. As the women gently braided our hair, our imaginations raced back to fairy-tale land! I felt like Rapunzel. As I looked at my cousins, I imagined Inaya was Belle and Ariana was Ariel. The cool breeze in the hot sun was refreshing, just as the whole ambience had been thus far. Now I could relate to the photos I had seen of my mom with an African hairdo in her photo album.

Soon some boats with freshly caught fish came onto land, and the fisherman were approaching us and other tourists to sell their catch. We looked at the beautiful fresh catch but of course could not buy it. Instead, we splurged on buying colorful African tops from these lovely ladies. I will never forget one of these ladies, whose name was Daisy. Daisy was beautiful and reminded me of the Egyptian queen Nefertiti. My mom, Farina, and Aunt Naz exchanged telephone numbers with Daisy, hoping to meet her someday again soon.

We rushed back to our rooms to change because we were going to meet someone very special in the city of Mombasa that day. It would be my mother's uncle, fondly known as Chacha, who is also the closest relative to being a grandpa for me, as I have never seen either of my grandfathers. My dad explained that we would also visit Old Town Mombasa.

After a long drive, we got onto the connecting Likoni Ferry that crossed the Kilindini Harbour to take us to the town.

The roads were extremely narrow, crowded, and a little bumpy. However, every building was rock-solid brick and stone and told the tale of the old British Empire that my parents had so often talked to me about. The paint on the buildings, however, had become tarnished and muddy over the years. There were people walking in long, loose robes, some selling fresh coconuts and fruits that we would never have seen back in the United States.

We stopped at the central pharmacy and parked our vehicles. Everyone was so excited because many of the adults had not seen Chacha in more than twenty years. There he sat, so tall, and I could immediately see a resemblance to my maternal grandpa, whose photographs I had seen in my mother's wallet. Everyone hugged and sat next to him on a sofa and chatted.

Uncle Amir got his camera out and shot these rather memorable moments. No one noticed how time fled and soon we waved goodbye to Chacha. Later we decided to walk around the town and also made a stopover for a light lunch snack at Blue Post Restaurant, which Nana highly recommended. I liked their meat samosas and ice-cream shake the best. We later visited the local fruit and produce market.

It was filled with stalls of different fruits and vegetables and even had a seafood area. Passion fruits and custard apples, also known as *sitaphal*, were everyone's favorites. The hawkers would cut the passion fruit in half and sprinkle it with a dab of a salt-and-red-chili mixture. It was sheer heaven to taste if you could handle the chilies.

As I walked beside my parents in this large market with very tall ceilings, my imagination took off ... I imagined myself in the olden days when the Arab influence in Mombasa would have been strong. My bedtime stories from *Arabian Nights*, *Aladdin and the Lamp*, and *Ali Baba and the Forty Thieves* came alive in my mind. I could see myself bargaining with the hawkers who, in fact, may have been the gang members of the forty thieves. I questioned their every move and gesture and pretended to talk on an imaginary phone with the police ... This was beginning to feel real.

"Sarah let's go," my dad called, pulling me out of my imaginary dream world. He was holding out his hand so that we could start for Old Town. Once in Old Town, the scene changed. The streets were very narrow and crowded with high side walls. The buildings and architecture were very Arabian, and while nothing seemed to have had any touch-ups, there was a solid look to everything. There was a mix of Arabian and Indian cultures, and the aroma of different foods filled the air.

We walked through the old, narrow brick alleys to reach the old fish market. The market was huge and looked like it was on top of a hill. The uphill climb was very tough, and there was also a very strong fish odor all around. Later we had to climb many flights of stairs to get inside the market and then to go down just as many stairs to get to the docking area behind the market. It was different from anything that the ASI sisters had seen. The drivers explained that this was where the boats would bring their catch for sale at the market every day.

While we enjoyed taking pictures, the strong fish smell was getting harder to bear. We were going to make a pit stop at the famous old lighthouse along Mama Ngina Drive, which is known for street foods. There was a huge parking lot bordering the sea and next to the lighthouse with numerous stalls selling varieties of snacky foods. We parked our cars, and everyone got out.

A young man was serving fresh fried cassava, which was first split across the middle and then sprinkled with salt, red chilies, and fresh squeezed lime juice. This was entirely new to me, and I was sold! Someone was also selling fried cassava chips doused with the same ingredients. The ASI team tried a small portion of everything. My dad was trying out the roasted corn, and his drink was fresh coconut juice. Mamu was relishing the fried cassava chips. Aunty Naz loved the roasted sweet corn. Nana was enjoying every bit of what is known as "*heart of palm.*" This is the core of the palm trunk, which is eaten raw and cut in slices. It tastes like coconut but has the crispiness of bamboo shoot. Uncle Amir savored a bit of everything. He was also not letting his camera miss a single moment.

The drivers mentioned that there was more to eat and sample on Makadara Street, but due to time constraints, we could not visit. After this rather hot afternoon in the tropical heat of Old Town Mombasa, we headed back to our resort to rest a little before getting out for a very special dinner, which I was told would be a highlight of the Mombasa trip.

After relaxing in the balcony of our rooms and chasing away the monkeys that were busy trying to come in, my dad sat beside me and told me the story of Ali Baba and the forty thieves.

I wasn't sure why he was doing that and wondered if he had read my mind earlier in the marketplace. But it felt right because this was a coast where the Omani Arabs had long lived and shared a very Arabic and Swahili culture.

Everyone dressed up for dinner, and I wondered why. The drive to the restaurant was not as long as I had expected. Soon we arrived at what appeared to look like a small house on the outside that had the words *Ali Barbour's* printed out on a signpost above the main entrance. We entered through the main door, and then our jaws dropped in both shock and awe. We had entered a huge cave that had stairs leading down to its bottom. This was an exclusive cave restaurant. Yes, it was a real cave that was thought to be 180,000 years old and was thirty-three feet underground.

The restaurant had been built within the cave's own natural environment. When the waters on the shoreline at some point dried out and the tides never rose that high again, this cave was discovered and turned into a five-star restaurant called Ali Barbour's to give it a touch of both the exotic and adventure from the tales of Ali Baba and the forty thieves.

There are a couple of levels within the restaurant with stairs, and the only man-made item are the floors. On a moonlit night, one can see the stars and the sky above through a ceiling, which is a hole in the middle of the cave. I kept wondering what would happen if it rained. True enough, it started to rain, and we were worried that we would get soaked. But I was fascinated to see a retractable ceiling slide right in to close off the hole.

Ali Barbour's is a seafood restaurant, and so our table splurged in ordering almost all the main entrees. I stuck with garlic shrimp with rice, while my two cousins split some grilled fish and sides of vegetables with their parents. All three of us were more interested in exploring the cave and hoping to find our own story. Perhaps someone hiding in a large pot? No, that would be too scary. We laughed and giggled and enjoyed each other's company as the adults savored the fresh catch of the day.

It was a real treat. I could now see why Uncle Hamid, Aunty Naz, and Mama spoke proudly of their place of birth.

CHAPTER 16
Mombasa, Day Four

August 10, 2019

We were up late that morning and decided to enjoy the pool for the most part of the morning. In the afternoon, Nabeel decided to teach the ASI team how to surf and ride the waves. We spent some time enjoying this treat with our precious Mamu, who is a brother, a best friend, and the kindest human being all rolled into one. Although I did not particularly like the feel of salt water in my nose, I stuck it out and enjoyed the waves.

No one wanted lunch because breakfast had been heavy. To our joy and surprise, a Jet Ski adventure had been arranged for us. We had instructors who rode along with us. As I rode on mine, I felt a thrill like never before, and the cool spray of water all over my face was a gift in the hot sun.

Unfortunately, the engine of my Jet Ski slowed down due to some fault or low battery, and the instructor had to keep switching it back on. I ended up having one of the longest rides. When I got back, my dad was relieved to see me. My two cousins and my mom also had a lot of fun with their Jet Skis.

Later, just walking on the shores of the ocean and collecting shells made me connect even deeper with Mama. After a short nap, the hustle and bustle were back.

Mama and Aunty Naz were reminiscing over their times in Mombasa when Mama had just graduated from medical school and had been treated to a grand holiday on the coast. They seemed to be talking about a dhow ride.

The drive to the dinner venue was long. Along the way, the other SUV that Alfred was driving hit something, and we saw them make a sudden stop. There on the road was a large cow that looked badly injured. Unfortunately, the poor animal had been hit by the SUV. I put my hands over my eyes, and tears started to brim. *The poor animal*, I thought. John was also very upset but mentioned how common such incidents were on these roads. As for the cow, if too badly wounded, it would probably be put to sleep. The adults in both cars were trying to cheer each other up and the children, but nothing they said seemed to help.

As we arrived at the harbor, we were ushered into the famous Tamarind Hotel where we would soon be picked up for dinner and a ride on the grand and famous old Tamarind dhow. This is a traditional Arab sailing boat which in the past served as a cargo trading boat. It had been turned into an exotic sailing restaurant.

The sunset was beautiful, throwing a splash of red, orange, and yellow on the hotel's elegant terrace, and everyone enjoyed posing for pictures.

Although the idea of a tour in an old-fashioned open Tamarind dhow sounded awesome, I was in no shape for this at all. My whole body was on fire, and my head hurt. As we boarded the dhow and were seated at the dinner table, the worst kind of seasickness set in! *Oh no*, I thought to myself. *This could ruin everyone's evening, especially Dad's.*

I clung to him as tightly as possible to help the pain, but it was no use. I was not able to look at, let alone eat, any of the delicacies set before us. Somehow, the cool breeze of the Indian

Ocean as the dhow gently swayed on the water was calming, and I rested in my dad's lap with my head on his shoulder. The rest of the family members were engaged in conversation and some listened to the soothing background music as they savored every course that was served at dinner. My aunt and Nana were engaged in conversation with some of the other guests who were also re-visiting Kenya.

By the time we finished the boat tour, it was past midnight. The experience was so unique that time had stood still, and nothing seemed to matter. I already felt much better.

Alas, everything must come to an end, and we were back in our hotel rooms. One thought stood out very clearly in all of our minds and conversations: this was the last night in Mombasa. I was overcome with nostalgia and the thought that I was going to say goodbye to this most enigmatic land of love and wonders brought tears to my eyes.

The breakfast was rushed and simple. The airport was small, and I had mixed feelings when I boarded a small aircraft for our flight back to Nairobi. It was once again pleasant to experience the hospitality of the hostesses and Mombasa people. They were efficient, polite, and welcoming. The ASI actually joked that these people seemed to belong to another world.

Once we got back into Nairobi, it felt almost like being home again. We had a new driver, but we all sorely missed Alfred and John, the two amazing guides who had toured us around for the entire three-week safari, keeping us well-informed about the local politics, news, each part of the game reserves, the different types of soil in different regions where we had traveled, the amazing animals, and the landscape. It had not only been a tour full of fun, relaxation, and entertainment, but it had been very educational.

CHAPTER 17
Back to Nairobi, Day One

August 11, 2019

The Highlight in Nairobi was lunch at the Carnivore Restaurant. I had heard about the mysterious, exotic game meat dishes served here from my mum. And now I was at this huge place, the house of authentic ensemble and entrees of zebra, lamb, ostrich, alligator, and many more. I was fascinated by the thought of the place but enjoyed my regular steak and chicken. The waiters served us different varieties of meat on skewers throughout the evening. The meat was served with an assortment of homemade sauces including mint, chili, and other flavors.

After lunch, we were in for yet another treat. The van drove us through miles of lush green countryside outside the city toward Kileleshwa, and there was a twinkle in my mom's eyes with a large grin on Aunty Naz's, Nana's, and Daddy's faces. When we arrived at the address, it was as though we had driven to a gated community of massive castles with iron gates that were closed. Etched into the large emblem on the gates were three words, *Servire Est Regnare*, along with a dragon.

This was Mama's school! I remember her singing the tune explaining that it was a hymn translated from Latin to English as, "God give us grace to serve Thee." This hymn was sung every evening before supper at the school. My mother pleaded with the security guard at the gates to let us in, but the constant answer was no because it was a weekend. An hour later, she came back to the bus with both tears and a grin on her face.

"She should have been a politician," Rimma said.

Mother had managed to speak with the head of security of the school, who, after all the necessary checks, had agreed to let us have a brief tour of the entire school. The tour enabled us to envision how Mama would have spent each day as a boarder in this magnificent environment. The tour lasted for more than two hours, and then we were escorted back to our van.

I was in a trance from what I had just experienced. I played on the same grand piano in the impressive school chapel that Mama had once played. We walked up the grand steps leading to the chapel and dining room, which were bordered by the expanse of green gardens and towering baronial boarding house buildings resembling castles, in which my mother had once lived. The experience had been nothing short of being in a fairy tale.

My imagination was taking off again when Aunty Naz pointed out that we were getting close to Aunt Pini's residence where another elaborate dinner awaited us. This would be our last evening to see some family members.

CHAPTER 18
Nairobi, Day Two

August 12, 2019

The next day was our last day in Nairobi, so we decided to tour the town and special places in Nairobi. On the list were a visit to Oshwal High School, where my aunt Naz had taught for more than a decade as a high school teacher. The moment Aunty Naz walked onto the grounds, it seemed like everyone knew her. The secretary, the teachers, and even the headmistress remembered her contribution in theater and English language. She had been a favorite of the students and her colleagues, having choreographed numerous plays and even acted herself on the national level. I felt so proud of dear Aunt Naz who is also like a godmother to me. I could feel her emotions the whole time.

Not so far from there was the Oshwal Girls School that Farina had attended, and we visited there too. She showed us places where the students would perch on a wall and have a snack. She called it her quiet spot. Uncle Amir drew out his camera, and we all posed for pictures.

The afternoon was spent bargaining and shopping for souvenirs in the local open-air flea market, also known as the Maasai Market. This was a unique shopping experience, and I would like to think of it as a wooden-and-tin mall with cloth barriers between stalls of colorful handmade goods, including jewelry, beaded bowls, pots and pans, curios, paintings, straw hats, baskets, leather sandals, belts, keychains, Maasai beads, and what have you. I wanted to buy *everything*, and the ASI sisters were in agreement with me. However, we were reminded about overweight luggage constraints.

Everyone was famished. The Westgate shopping mall was not far, and we soon found ourselves sitting at a table in Nana's favorite coffee spot in this mall, the Dorman's Coffee Shop. Their tuna salad Niçoise, chicken pies, croissants, and pastries were amazing. The adults kept raving about the coffee and especially the cappuccino. We then all bought beautiful table mats, coasters, and trivets at an exotic souvenir shop in the mall.

Although we had all enjoyed ourselves thoroughly, there was a certain sadness too.

The ASI sisters walked with their giant ice creams and hugged each other knowingly. Tomorrow we would be back on a plane to the United States, our home.

CHAPTER 19
Flight Back to the United States

August 13, 2019

On the flight back, I remembered all the exotic animals. I could not help but draw them out in my sketchbook, thinking about all the small details. I was awakened from a quick nap by the flight attendant who brought me my dinner. The tray was full of fruits and vegetables. The main course looked like spaghetti with meatballs, and the dessert tasted like chocolate heaven.

"It's a chocolate lava cake with vanilla ice cream!" exclaimed Ariana.

When I finished eating, I watched a movie about Kenya's animals and resorts. The ASI planned their second trip to Kenya. Nana had shared many of his personal videos with us and we recalled seeing him in places such as Muranga, Kisi, Kisumu and Nyeri which had not been possible to visit in this short trip…. certainly those could be the reason for a return trip. For some reason, I could not let go of this trip.

Printed in the United States
by Baker & Taylor Publisher Services